SOUTHERN EMUs IN COLOUR

includes Electric Locomotives

JOHN C. MORGAN

IAN ALLAN Publishing

First published 1994

ISBN 0 7110 2318 2

© Ian Allan Ltd 1994

Designed by Alan C. Butcher

Published by Ian Allan Publishing

an imprint of Ian Allan Ltd, Terminal House, Station Approach, Shepperton, Surrey TW17 8AS; and printed by Ian Allan Printing Ltd, Coombelands House, Coombelands Lane, Addlestone, Weybridge, Surrey KT15 1HY.

All photographs are by the author except where otherwise shown.

Previous page:
The two cows by Valebridge Crossing are totally disinterested in 4COR No 3154 forming a stopping service from Brighton to Haywards Heath on a fine 24 August evening, in 1972. This was the service that used to run through to Horsted Keynes until closure of that branch in October 1963.

Front cover:
The 4CEP units were built quicker than they could be used (they were actually ordered in time for a new scheme!), and as the Horsted Keynes branch was being worked as a single line by this time (17 May 1959), the other line was used to store upwards of 30 units before moving to the South East Division for the Kent Coast electrification. *R. C. Riley*

Rear cover:
4CAP unit No 3202 stands in the down platform at Gillingham on 12 September 1991. The CAPs were formed of two 2HAP units coupled semi-permanently with the first class compartments declassified, and were originally intended for Coastway traffic, hence the 'C'. The interior ends of each 2HAP were painted black to appear similar to normal intermediate coach ends. *R. C. Riley*

Below:
Now classed as 930s, Deicing/Sandite units stand in the siding at Chart Leacon Depot just north of Ashford on 7 September 1990. No 008 rebuilt from 2EPB stock has just received an NSE repaint, and shows its headlights fitted to enable the driver to pick up the yellow trackside indications to start and terminate the use of the equipment particularly at night. *R. C. Riley*

Introduction

'Southern Electric' — a poignant phrase for all who over the years of this century have had cause to travel by train south of the Thames. It must conjure up a variety of thoughts — affection, loathing, a necessary evil, a means to get to work, a day trip to the coast, the distinctive smell of the old electric motors, the exhausting of the braking system, the flashing across the sky on a frosty night.....

My first recollection is of eight-coach trains formed of two 3-car SUB units with two trailer coaches sandwiched between them, passing through Cheam, my home in the days during and after the war. Also remembered are the bull-nosed SUB units of ex-LSWR design with the one large open compartment twice the size of normal ones, in which I travelled to visit my grandmother in Twickenham. Many books have been produced with black and white photographs of not only that era, but of earlier and more recent days. However, very few publications have ventured into colour photographs of Southern Electrics, and the present work seeks to redress the balance by a small amount. Throughout the book, I have used the old standard designation of unit classes well known to Southern enthusiasts and railwaymen alike, namely 1 figure/3 letters (eg 4REP), the figure indicating the number of coaches in the unit. This is rather more descriptive than the somewhat featureless computer numbering system in current use.

My own colour photography commenced in late 1960, using an Agfa Super-Silette 35mm camera with Prontor SVS shutter and Agfa CT18 100 ASA film. Light readings were taken initially with a Sixtry lightmeter, followed some 10 years later by the inevitable Weston Master. The first change was from Agfa film to Fuji RD100 (again 100 ASA rating) in April 1972. The shutter of the poor old Super-Silette finally gave up the ghost in late 1980, and the replacement was the present Pentax MX body with standard Pentax 50mm lens and 70-210mm telephoto. The last change was in approximately 1985 when the ASA rating of RD100 appeared to alter and, since then, RH135 of 400 ASA has been used. All photographs are by the author except where otherwise shown.

I should emphasise that a number of the photographs in this book have been taken from what I would call privileged positions. As a railwayman myself, my job has taken me on or about the track as a matter of course, and this will explain the camera position in those cases. However, I would be one of the first to point out that nearly all could have been taken from places accessible to the general public, and indeed it will be seen how many are actually taken from station platforms or convenient overbridges. Again, as a railwayman, I must underline the dangers of trespass, and would add that even railwaymen suffer accidents in just being on or about the track.

The intention in preparation of this work was to show as many different types of stock and liveries as possible that were extant in either Southern Railway or Southern Region days, and in that context, I am particularly grateful to colleague Phil Evans and the two well-known railway photographers Brian Morrison and Dick Riley who have supplied extra material. My thanks go also to Simon Forty, Peter Waller and their team at Ian Allan for their help and advice.

I would acknowledge using information from other Ian Allan publications — various ABCs, Moody's *Southern Electric*, Behrend's *Pullman in Europe*, Colin Marsden's two volume *Southern Electric Multiple-Units*, and Dendy Marshall's *Southern Railway*.

John C. Morgan,
Lindfield, West Sussex, March 1994.

Pre-Nationalisation Designs

First in the series, 6PUL No 3001 (originally numbered 2001), approaches Wivelsfield with an up working on Saturday morning, 19 February 1966. These units were built during 1932 for the opening of the main line Brighton/Worthing electrification, and were only replaced by the coming of the CIGs and BIGs soon after this picture was taken.

6PUL (one Pullman coach in a 6-car set) unit No 3006 comes off the Eastbourne line at Keymer Junction leading the 14.00 Ore-Victoria on 11 August 1963. The Pullman car is named 'Rose'. The footbridge at Junction Road level crossing in the left background has since been removed.
1/250, f2.8.

The Brighton electrification utilised initially 6PUL units for the
fast trains, and when the third-rail reached Eastbourne, 6PAN sets
were introduced. One of each became the standard formation, and
an example is shown here approaching Keymer Junction just south
of Wivelsfield with 6PUL No 3011 leading. The date is
15 September 1963, the day that the LSWR 'T9' No 120 and the
Caledonian Single No 123 brought a special to the Bluebell line.
1/500, f3.5.

The 4LAV units inaugurated the Brighton electrification in 1933. Here No 2952 stands in the Down platform at Hassocks on 11 April 1964. The change in width of the motor coaches behind the guard's compartment is clearly visible. The LBSCR platform awning and roof behind the train was blown down one night in the 1970s, and had to be demolished; hence today's somewhat spartan substitute. *1/250, f4.*

4LAV No 2926 approaches Wivelsfield on 2 September 1967.
The 4LAVs were built in 1931/2 for the Brighton main line
electrification inaugurated on the first day of 1933 to be used
largely on the semi-fast trains, and were retired only when the
4VEPs took over stopping and semi-fast services.

1/250, f3.5.

On a fine summer morning, 23 July 1966, two 4LAV units, with No 2949 leading, approach Burgess Hill on a London Bridge-Brighton semi-fast service. The appearance of the cutting slopes with the telegraph pole run and the short grass would not be recognised today — full grown trees and bushes now cover the area. With the decrease in staffing levels of track staff and the increase in mechanised maintenance from the 1960s onwards, trees were allowed to grow up on the lineside — now environmentalists complain to the railways when they attempt to cut them back, and 'leaves on the line' is the result!
1/500, f3.5.

A well filled train of four 2BILs heads south from Clapham
Junction on 10 September 1961. The Brighton line can be seen
converging on the extreme right of the picture. The 2BILs were
built in the mid-1930s for various work such as Maidstone, Sussex
Coast, Ascot etc, and shared much of their work after the war with
the 2HALs. *R. C. Riley*

2BIL No 2019 approaches Wivelsfield on a down Victoria-Brighton stopping service in the last months before the 4VEPs finally took over this route. The second 2BIL unit has an 'all-over' yellow front end. It is a fine Saturday morning — 3 May 1969. *1/500, f3.5.*

Danger
Do not touch
live rail

Passengers must
not cross the line

Left:
Preserved 2BIL No 2090 heads 4SUB No 4732 across Ditchling Common towards Lewes on 30 September 1984 with a special organised by the Southern Electric Group. The yellow end panels rather detract from the otherwise original livery, but the green stirs the memories of many a commuter of years ago.

Above:
Preserved 2BIL No 2090 coupled to the 4SUB No 4732 passes the LBSCR signalbox at the east end of Lewes station on Saturday 21 September 1991 as part of the celebrations for 'Brighton 150'. The BILs were constructed between 1935 and 1938, No 2090 being one of the later ones. The double junction immediately beneath the front of the train had recently been relaid with new types of crossings; this is where the line from Brighton meets that from Keymer Junction.

Left:
2HAL unit No 2602 heads north from platform 2 at Three Bridges on 6 May 1961, passing the LBSCR water crane still extant on the platform end. Keen trainspotters on platform 3 (standing by an Exmouth Junction Concrete Works SR lamp-post) record the unit numbers. There would also seem to be a railwayana collector's dream on the same platform, with Southern green signs in evidence!
1/500, f2.8.

Right:
Seen at a location instantly recognisable to preservationists, 2HAL No 2674 forms the stopping service from Horsted Keynes to Seaford via Haywards Heath when the Ardingly branch was still open, providing a direct BR connection to the Bluebell Railway. The date is 15 September 1963, the day that the Caledonian Single and the LSWR 'T9' brought a special to Haywards Heath for through running on to the Bluebell line.
1/250, f5.

On display during the National Railway Museum on Tour
exhibition at Swindon, resplendent in Southern Railway livery, is
the bull-nosed LSWR 3SUB motor coach No 8143, unit No 1293.
It was photographed on 13 April 1990, the 'H' headcode
indicating Waterloo-Hampton Court, or to Weybridge via
Hounslow. *Alan C. Butcher*

Left:
Reformed in 1945/6, 4SUB No 4337 consisted of a 1925-built 3SUB with an additional steel trailer. The motor coach is seen standing outside the original electric car repair sheds at Peckham Rye, built by the LBSCR for their 6.7kV overhead electrification in about 1909. No 4337 was photographed from a stationary passing train(!) on 3 November 1962. *1/60, f5.*

Right:
Just before lunch on 27 August 1982, 4SUB No 4738 is seen leaving the South Eastern side of Victoria on a Central Division service. It will cross to the Down Brighton Slow some 200m further on, and climb Grosvenor Bank to cross the Thames. The impressive roof over platforms 1-8 can be seen behind Eccleston Bridge.

17

Left:
4SUB No 4501 passes under an Up steam train to Victoria at the intersection bridge at what was then Queens Road Battersea (now Queenstown Road). The 'V' headcode indicates a 'Kingston Roundabout' — Waterloo to Waterloo via Kingston and Twickenham. The date is 26 July 1959. *R. C. Riley*

Below left:
4SUB No 4551 with its intermediate steel trailer coach leaves Tulse Hill with a West Croydon-Holborn Viaduct service on the morning of 3 June 1956. Southern Railway semaphore signals are much in evidence at the far end of the station where the line splits three ways — to Crystal Palace, Streatham, and Streatham Hill. *R. C. Riley*

Right
4COR No 3145 emerges from Clayton Tunnel on an Up Brighton-Haywards Heath all stations service on 22 August 1972. Often known as 'Nelson' stock from the one-eyed look of the front end, the opposite side from the driver showing the route indication, these units were built essentially for the Portsmouth Direct and the Portsmouth via mid-Sussex lines in 1937/8 together with their complementary 4RES units.

6COR unit No 3049 stands in the Down Siding adjacent to Stewarts Lane Depot, with Battersea Power Station still alive in the background. The 6CORs were made up from displaced 6PAN and 6PUL Brighton line sets from the end of 1965, to be used for a limited time as relief services from Victoria to the Kent Coast. No 3049 was photographed on 28 March 1968.
P. J. Evans

A classic picture of 4SUB No 4506 passing Clapham Cutting on 24 May 1958. What days these were — a very full telegraph route, and allotments totally unfenced right down to the track cess! Only one of the four tracks had been laid with flat bottom rail by this period. *R. C. Riley*

'Brighton Belle'

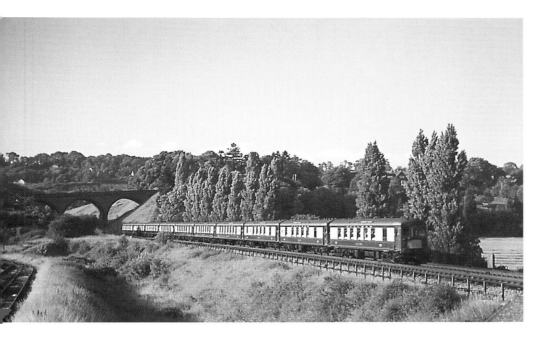

Left:
At the end of the 1960s, it was decided to refurbish the three 5BEL sets, resulting in them being painted in the blue/grey livery of the period. Here No 3052 and 4BUF No 3076 form a somewhat unconventional 'Brighton Belle' working through Wandsworth Common in April 1969. *Frank Hornby/Colour-Rail (DE337)*

Above:
Photographed on the last day of timetabled services, 30 April 1972, the interior of a 1st class Pullman car on the 'Brighton Belle' unit 5BEL No 3053 is seen here in all its full glory. The superb woodwork, the individual chairs, and even the Pullman coat of arms over the doorway, all point to the uniqueness and opulence of these trains.

Post-Nationalisation Designs

Left:
The prototype 1956 built 4BEP unit No 7001 is seen heading the 10.00 Victoria-Brighton non-stop just south of Wivelsfield on a bright Saturday morning, 19 March 1967. This was the day that the last steam locomotive travelled down the Brighton line (until recently) — 'West Country' Pacific No 34108 *Wincanton.* *1/500, f3.5.*

Right:
Green 4CIG No 7303 was the only unit to be painted with a wrap-round yellow end, and it is seen here stopping at Wivelsfield, on 2 September 1967. It appears that the station staff had not been along to extinguish their gas lamps yet that morning! *1/250, f3.5.*

Left:
Seen through the doorway of Coulsdon North Signalbox just before its demolition under the Brighton Line Resignalling Scheme is 4CIG No 7363 on a Brighton semi-fast heading down the Quarry line in May 1984. To the right are the original lines via Redhill which rejoin the Quarry lines just behind the train at the charmingly named Stoats Nest Junction. The accident at this site of an Up express in January 1910 killed the author's wife's great uncle who was standing on the platform at the time.

Right:
Outside the old Gloucester Road Junction SB just north of East Croydon a 4CIG on the 11.51 Eastbourne waits while a Class 73 overtakes on the slow line with a 'Gatwick Express' on Friday 31 May 1985. The two double junctions below the bridge where the 4 CIG is standing were colloquially known as Glory Hole Junction. The Crystal Palace television mast is on the skyline.

Left:
Taken on the same visit to Valebridge Crossing as the 4COR on page1, this shot shows 4CIG No 7364 on a Victoria to Brighton semi-fast, a 12-car rake with a 4VEP in the middle. Having travelled in these units for some 30 years as a commuter, the author calculates that he has spent one full year (365 days, 24 hours) sitting in these trains!

Above:
4BIG No 7044 takes a 12-car Eastbourne train south from Haywards Heath on Saturday lunchtime, 16 April 1983. The buffet version of the CIG stock is famous for the provision of hot buttered toast, not generally available anywhere else on the BR system these days! The foreground is now part of the extensive commuter car park.

Left:
On the morning of 3 October 1984, everything seemed to be heading south from East Croydon at the same time. On the left is the VSOE Pullman stock behind a Class 33 on the Down Slow line, while in the centre 4BIG No 7054 brings up the rear of a 12-coach train crossing on to the Reversible. On the right GLV No 9109 contributes power to the 6-coach 'Gatwick Express', on the Down Fast line. Waiting in the distance on the Up Slow is a 4EPB unit.

Below:
Two 4VEP units, No 7814 leading, approaching Clapham Junction on a Waterloo-Dorking working at lunchtime on an April day in 1984. The yellow 60 cut-out sign near the rear of the train indicates the speed restriction for the Up Fast line towards Queenstown Road — these signs were changed to road style signs (black numeral on white circular background) in early NSE days, not a vast improvement in view of the need for cleaning and keeping free from graffiti!

Left:
Seen through the overbridge at the north end of Burgess Hill station is 4VEP No 7806 on an Up stopping service to Victoria on the morning of 25 April 1981.

Below left:
A contrast in liveries — the early NSE red, white and blue, with the sharp angle corners on 4VEP No 7850, and the 'Jaffa-cake' colouring on an unidentified 4CEP inviting one to 'ride the 1066 electrics' on the Hastings line, stand coupled together at Cannon Street on 23 August 1986.
R. C. Riley

Right:
Leaning out of the window of the old closed (and since demolished) Victoria Eastern Signalbox then used as a conference room produced this view of recently refurbished 4CEP No 1576 on the morning of 27 August 1982. In the early 1980s, hopper ventilators replaced the traditional steam type sliding windows in the CEPs and BEPs, less comfortable seats replaced the more luxuriant previous style particularly in the first class, and modern lighting and tinted windows were provided.

33

Below:
Refurbished 4CEP No 1570, and BR type 4EPB No 5627 stand at Stewarts Lane Depot on 4 September 1990. The Kent Coast logo is on the side of No 5627, and the NSE livery shows the darker (more attractive) later blue, in contrast to the lighter blue on the 4VEP unit behind. The later curved bottom edges to the colour changes can be contrasted with those on the 4VEP shown on page 32. The red/blue/grey logo is also in evidence on the front of both units.
R. C. Riley

Right:
Autumn 'Jaffa-cake'. 4CEP No 1558 forms the 16.50 Victoria-Ramsgate on 14 November 1990. With Shortlands station in the background, it is on the crossover designed by the author soon after he started working for the Southern Region in 1974!
B. Morrison

On a bright 25 September morning in 1986, two 'Jaffa-cake'-liveried 4CEPs stand in platform 5 at Charing Cross, while 4EPB No 5242 waits at platform 3. This view is now completely changed with the commercial development that has taken place over the top of the station.

A study in green front ends! At lunchtime on 4 August 1962,
4CEP No 7135 waits to take the Fast Up to Charing Cross from
Ramsgate. In the platform behind can be seen 2EPB No 5618 on
the left and 2EPB No 5623 in the centre (both to SR design).
1/125, f7.

A 12-car train headed by SR-designed 2EPB No 5614 with BR
type 2EPB behind climbs Grosvenor Bank outside Victoria *en
route* for the Kent Coast on 10 September 1960. Two 2BIL units
wait to enter Victoria over on the Brighton side. The 2 and 4EPBs
were the successors to the NOLs and SUBs, first appearing in
1951, and are only now being finally replaced by the Networkers.
R. C. Riley

A late afternoon Waterloo-Guildford via Cobham train approaches Vauxhall on what was then known as the Down Main Through — now the Down Fast. It is formed of 4EPB No 5319, a BR rather than Southern-designed unit. The Victoria Tower and part of the clock tower at the Palace of Westminster can be seen above the train. *1/250, f3.5.*

A portrait of 4EPB No 5036 standing in the early winter sunshine in the stabling siding at the London end of Maidstone East on 22 November 1981. The leaves were late in falling that year.

4EPB No 5264 has just left Blackfriars (visible behind the last coach), and is heading for Holborn Viaduct over Ludgate Hill Junction on Wednesday 18 March 1987. This junction was the divergence of the Thameslink line down to Farringdon and King's Cross, and was moved to a position some 150m behind the camera on 1 May 1988 to facilitate staging works for the abolition of Holborn Viaduct. It was then renamed Apothecary Street Junction; this was also removed at Easter 1989 when Great Victoria Street bridge at the rear of the train was lowered at the end nearest to the camera by one metre to give a gradient of 1 in 29 down to the new St Paul's (now City Thameslink) station.

Shunting on 24 October 1985 into the Carriage Sidings on the
Windsor side at Clapham Junction is 2EPB No 6327, one of the
SR design build of 1953. This is one of 15 2EPBs to have bars put
on the door droplights, for use on the North London Line from
Richmond to North Woolwich. Two destination boards can be
seen by the driver's windows. Clapham Junction 'A' signalbox is
in the background.

The 4REPs were built as tractor units for the Bournemouth Electrification; they were designed to haul two 4TC trailer units which were then taken on to Weymouth by Class 33 diesels. Each 4REP had a similar power rating to a Class 55 'Deltic'. The Southern Electric Group have run many special trains over the years, one such being the 'Wenceslas Wanderer' when they persuaded the South Western Division to part with a 4REP, No 3008, on 3 December 1983. It was parked in the Down Goods Loop at Sittingbourne while participants on the tour visited the Sittingbourne & Kemsley Light Railway. Standing in the Down Loop platform about to leave for Sheerness was 4VEP No 7776. *S. J. Pearce*

Taken from the window of the already defunct and now demolished Wimbledon 'C' signalbox, some half-a-mile to country from Wimbledon station, an 8-car rake is seen of the first Southern electric units not to have acquired a 3-letter class description. The 4-car 508s were the first production main line sliding door stock on the Southern, introduced in 1979, but have since been moved to Merseyside as 3-car sets. Each surplus coach was incorporated into the second batch of Class 455 units (see page 46). No 508024 was bound for Hampton Court at lunchtime on 13 September 1983.

In October 1987, unit No 5850 of the first series of Class 455
stands in platform 5 at East Croydon forming a London Bridge to
Caterham service. The old platform awnings shown here have now
been replaced as part of the complete rebuilding of the station. The
early NSE livery here has sharp angles between colours, rather than
the later rounded corners.

Below:
Class 455 No 5705 pulls out of platform 4 at Waterloo on an early evening train to Hampton Court on 14 March 1985. This photograph shows clearly the different shape of the second coach in the unit — one of the otherwise redundant Class 508 coaches when 3-car sets were transferred to Merseyside. This fourth coach of each set was incorporated into the 455/7s. 4CIG No 7357 waits to leave platform 5 for the Portsmouth via Cobham line.

Right:
Class 455 No 5712 waits in the bay platform at Weybridge before heading for Staines via Addlestone. The March 1986 afternoon sun picks out the front end detail.

Non-Production Prototype EMUs, NPCCS and Departmentals

Left:
No Southern Electric book would be complete without the double-deck units designed by Bulleid, Nos 4001 and 4002. A freshly painted No 4001 with remarkably dirty front end rounds the seven chains radius curve by the signalbox at the approach to Cannon Street on 12 June 1959. The double track turning off to the right was singled under the London Bridge Resignalling Scheme in the mid 1970s, and forms the direct connection to Charing Cross (and Blackfriars) from Cannon Street. The four track section on which No 4001 is travelling from Borough Market Junction was also reduced to three tracks in 1991 because of clearance problems with the new Networker trains. *R. C. Riley*

Above:
Two 4-car units, Nos 4001 and 4002, were built as prototypes for sliding door stock, and ran for a short time on the South Eastern Division, before settling down to regular running on the South Western suburban area. Here, 4PEP No 4002 forms a Hampton Court service at Clapham Junction on 24 March 1976. *P. J. Evans*

Left:
Following their
introduction in 1971
for evaluation
purposes the
prototype sliding door
stock carried their
first fare-paying
passengers in June
1973. 4PEP No 4001
was photographed at
East Wimbledon
Depot on 24 February
1979, some 30 months
after withdrawal. The
production version
became the Class
508s which after
service on the
Southern, were moved
to the Liverpool area.
The Southern used the
numbers 4001/2
several times as a
coding for prototype
units. *Frank Hornby*

Right:
Departmental Stores
unit No 024 rebuilt
from postwar 4SUB
motor coaches takes
the Down Fast line at
Shortlands Junction
on 24 June 1976.
Stores trains run from
one depot to another
transferring various
renewable items to the
more outlying depots,
usually on a weekly
basis. *R. C. Riley*

Above left:
The first in a class of 10 MLVs, No 68001, later unit No 9001, is standing at Stewarts Lane Depot on 13 June 1959 soon after being built. They were constructed to take the boat train luggage right down to the quay particularly at Folkestone Harbour, and usually ran in pairs coupled to two CEPs and a BEP forming 14-coach trains, the longest regular Southern electric trains ever. *R. C. Riley*

Below left:
Thursday 12 September 1991. Two MLVs led by No 9004 head the water cart train from Ashford to Ramsgate Depot, seen here approaching Folkestone West. During the drought of 1991, water for carriage washing was obtained from an artesian well at Dover Priory and this was conveyed to Ramsgate and Ashford in these tank wagons. The MLVs carried many different liveries, starting with Southern Region green, but here in full NSE colours.

Right:
MLV No 9001, now known as No 931091, and previously as No 68001, stands on 5 May 1989 in platform 7 at Victoria in a short-lived livery of Post Office red — it was decided that they were too easy to recognise by potential thieves! The MLVs are probably second only to the Class 73s with regard to the number of different liveries they have carried. *R. C. Riley*

Southern Locomotives

Above:
The original of the three electric locomotives, No 20001 (ex-CC1 of 1941) stands in ex-works condition at Stewarts Lane Depot on 29 May 1968 in preparation for taking Her Majesty to the Derby at Epsom Racecourse two days later. Part of the front of 4EPB No 5214 is visible on the left. *P. J. Evans*

Right:
Originally built in 1943 as No CC2, the second of three electric locomotives built by the Southern Railway intended for heavy freight traffic is shown on display at an Open Day at Eastleigh Works on 5 August 1964. No 20002 along with her sisters performed much work in latter days on the Victoria-Newhaven boat trains.
1/125, f5.6.

Left:
No E5001 is on display in its original livery in what is now an historic location — the twin-turntabled building of the National Railway Museum at York. The Class 71 was built in 1959 for the Kent Coast electrification and intended for boat train and freight working, the pantograph being used in the sidings at Hither Green and other Eastern Section yards. Withdrawn as No 71001, it was photographed on 29 April 1980.

Below:
Electric locomotive No E5003 is seen backing down on to the parcels vans in London Bridge low level prior to forming the 12.44 to Ramsgate on 17 June 1959. Introduced this very year, these locomotives were built for the Kent Coast electrification principally to haul boat trains, but they were also used for parcels as shown. *R. C. Riley*

Left:
The very first Up electric 'Golden Arrow' left Dover Marine four minutes late at 18.17 on Monday 12 June 1961 behind No E5015 hauling two CCTs, eight Pullmans and two coaches. After five permanent way slowings and two signal stops, and a maximum of 83mph before Paddock Wood, arrival at Victoria was 13 minutes late at 20.03. The train is seen here at Dover Marine (now Western Docks) awaiting departure.
1/15, f2.8.

Below:
Standing in platform 7 at Brighton on 29 August 1967 is electro-diesel No E6003, now known as Class 73. There have probably been nearly as many Class 73 liveries as members of the class, and the early green/grey must rank as one of the most attractive. This locomotive is now operating on Merseyside.
1/15, f2.8.

Above:
Electro-diesel No E6013 in its early blue/grey livery stands in the Up-side yard at Redhill very early in the morning of 10 July 1967. These versatile locomotives have been the mainstay of Southern Region operating for more than 30 years, and indeed some have now moved to Merseyside to work out their days on the Wirral system.

Right:
In one of its many liveries over the years, No 73142 *Broadlands* approaches Ashford with the Down 'Venice-Simplon Orient Express' at lunchtime on 14 October 1983. The first Pullman coach is 'Minerva' built in 1927 by Midland Carriage & Wagon. This area is being completely remodelled again under the Ashford International station proposals, and the building on the right will be on the line of new tracks.

Below:
A somewhat dull June morning in 1981 has the royal train with No 73142 *Broadlands* in charge on a special working up from Gatwick Airport, approaching East Croydon. The multi-storey car park behind is built on the site of the old Fairfield Yard, where the short branch line (just 29 chains long) left the main line for Croydon Central.

Right:
On Derby Day 1987, an excessively smart (with regard to the pipework) No 73142 *Broadlands* takes Her Majesty the Queen through East Croydon towards Purley and the Tattenham Corner branch, in her own train. Noteworthy is the absence of any special lamps or discs on the front of the locomotive. A 4EPB unit passes behind.

Far left:
On the first Wednesday in June 1985, No 73129 propels an Up 'Gatwick Express' over Cottage Junction near Selhurst. This embankment was constructed in 1981 as part of the Brighton Line Resignalling Scheme flyover to enable slow line trains from Victoria to cross the London Bridge fast lines without conflicting movements. A 4EPB waits to enter Selhurst after the 'Gatwick Express' has passed.

Left:
Sweeping round the curve from Redhill Tunnel towards Earlswood, No 73212 *Airtour Suisse* heads a 6-coach 'Gatwick Express' on the afternoon of Saturday 3 March 1990. This curve was realigned in 1983/4 under the Brighton Line Resignalling Scheme to permit 80mph in lieu of the previous 60mph. It involved the demolition of the old LBSCR Earlswood Junction signalbox.

Left:
On 4 June 1982, No 73122 backs down from Stewarts Lane Depot into Victoria prior to taking that morning's 'Venice-Simplon Orient Express' to Folkestone Harbour. The number of different liveries that have been displayed on Class 73s runs well into double figures, and this all blue sides version was one of the most common, but the black roof was unusual.

Right:
The late LBSCR architecture of the ramps and the booking hall beyond of East Croydon station has now been swept away and replaced by a striking modern structure of cables and glass. On the morning of 15 September 1983, a spotless No 73121 stands at the country end of platform 4 having just been named *Croydon 1883-1983* at the other end of the platform by the lady mayor of the borough. In the presence of an extremely embarrassed SR General Manager, a very well briefed lady proceeded to comment on the fact that she was naming a 20-year-old locomotive that would in future be shooting straight through East Croydon on the 'Gatwick Express' trains without even stopping! She was given a cab-ride to the country end of the platform!

While delivery of the Class 442 electrics (5WES) for the Bournemouth line was taking place, 91 and 92 headcode (fast and semi-fast) trains ran as 7 or 8-coach rakes of 4TC/REP coaches behind or in front of two Class 73 electro-diesels. This was because the motors from the REPs were built into the new stock. Seen between Basingstoke and Hook, two different liveried '73s' form the 09.45 from Poole to Waterloo on Tuesday 5 July 1988.

No E6107 is seen standing in Clapham Junction yard on 11 September 1972. These electro-diesels had been rebuilt from surplus E50xx electric locomotives to haul the boat train services to Southampton Docks following electrification of the Bournemouth line in 1966. They were also used to Weymouth Quay, but with decreasing numbers of special boat trains, their lives were fairly short, their final numbering being in the 74xxx series.

Running Rights

Left:
Electric visitors to the Southern are indeed a rarity.
Ex-Metropolitan Railway, London Transport locomotive No 12
Sarah Siddons is posing for her portrait in platform 13 at London
Bridge after a gauging run from Wimbledon Park via St Helier,
Sutton and Streatham on Friday 6 July 1984. This was prior to
hauling the 'Mary Rose' from Waterloo to Portsmouth Harbour on
the following day.

Above:
After the previous day's gauging run, *Sarah Siddons* hauled the
'Mary Rose', an enthusiasts' special from Waterloo to Portsmouth
on Saturday 7 July 1984. A photographic run-past was arranged at
Havant where after backing out of the platform, the train ran
through on the Down Fast, before backing into the platform again
to pick up the participants.

'Underground' Electrics

Left:
Introduced in 1940, the stock for the Waterloo & City line has only recently been replaced. DMB No S60 is seen here in 1976 approaching the reversing siding at Waterloo, while the previous service train is half way out of the platform — the signal already returned to red. The rectangular building on the left is the signalbox. It is important to record that this photograph was taken with full knowledge and agreement of the train driver — flash photography can be blinding to drivers, and should be avoided for moving trains.

Right:
Along with virtually everything else, the Waterloo & City line stock succumbed to NSE livery. With No 60 nearest the camera a 5-car unit stands at Bank. *Colour-Rail (DE1155)*

Left:
On display at an Open Day in Brighton station on 30 June 1973 was the preserved Waterloo & City line electric shunter previously numbered DS75, and sporting its cycling lion emblem facing the heraldic wrong way! The locomotive had been used for moving stock on and off the Armstrong lift at Waterloo as well as for engineering trains down 'the drain'. Also on show that day at Brighton were steam locomotives Nos 30245, 30587, 33001, 34051 *Winston Churchill* and 45000, along with departmental emu No 053.

Right:
Ever since the start of electrification on the Isle of Wight, ex-London Transport tube trains have formed the rolling stock. The first series was formed of two types of set, the 4VEC and 3TIS. Forming the shuttle service between Ryde Pier Head and Esplanade is 4VEC unit No 485041 leading an unidentified 3TIS on 7 July 1984.

Below:
4VEC No 042 departs from Ryde Esplanade for Ryde Pier Head on 26 October 1971. These units were introduced with the Isle of Wight electrification in 1967, when also the main line was cut back to Shanklin instead of passing Wroxall and running under St Boniface Down to Ventnor.

Right:
Unit 4VEC No 485043 stops in the Up platform at Brading, with the rear two coaches newly painted in 'RydeRail' Network SouthEast livery. Built from 1923 onwards, these coaches virtually qualified for 'pre-grouping' status, and lasted right up to the end of the 1980s. Their replacements were 50 years young!

3TIS No 035 waits at Ryde Esplanade with the shuttle to Pier Head on 12 May 1979. The 4VEC and 3TIS units were reformed in 1985 into 5VEC and 2TIS to suit operating conditions — only one of these units remains, now a mere 70 years old! *R. C. Riley*

'The new Island Line trains are here' proclaims the banner on the lattice footbridge at Brading station where unit No 483001 forms a special from Ryde on 13 July 1989. Replacing the 4VEC/3TIS units, the Class 483s were also London Underground cast-offs — perhaps a little unfair, as they were considerably refurbished at Eastleigh before going across to Wight. However, the small wheels combined with track resting on rounded shingle do make for some lively riding qualities! *B. Morrison*

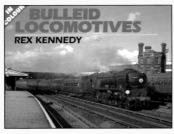